Jee Sun Kim

Jee Sun Kim

Ariel Star

iUniverse, Inc.
Bloomington

Jee Sun Kim

iUniverse books may be ordered through booksellers or by contacting:

iUniverse
1663 Liberty Drive
Bloomington, IN 47403
www.iuniverse.com
1-800-Authors (1-800-288-4677)

ISBN: 978-1-4620-5923-2 (sc)
ISBN: 978-1-4620-5924-9 (ebk)

Printed in the United States of America

iUniverse rev. date: 11/07/2011

CONTENTS

I was born in Seoul, South Korea. I was adopted when I was two years old. My Korean name was Jee Sun Kim.

I was diagnosed with Nervous Breakdown, Bipolar Disorder and Paranoid Schizophrenia in that order. I have been in and out of mental institutions at least 5 times in the past 2 years. I earned a Bachelors degree in Computer Engineering September 4th 2004.

Today is Friday, August 05, 2011. I am 18 weeks pregnant and 30 years old. It is my first baby and the first time I ever got pregnant. I was inspired to write this book because of Karen Arnold, Sam Williams and my baby.

After walking outside in my bra, underwear and winter coat, Karen said, "You could write a book about your life." I never really thought about it until Sam told me the same thing when I moved into my very first apartment. His eyes were bulging out of his head because he was so serious about it.

The psyche meds will deform the baby. I have stopped taking them. I was taking Ambilify, Depokote, and Lithium. Surprisingly, I am doing okay without them. I am taking a giant leap of faith. Everyone in my life told me to get an abortion. I am really scared that I am going to flip out without my medication. Part of me believes these diagnoses are bullshit and there is nothing wrong with me. Part of me thinks, "what if it is true."

This book will not be organized in chronological order. You will experience my thoughts as they come to me. Consider this book as a compilation of short stories. The short stories could be memories, a journal entry, my thoughts, feelings, reactions or an experience.

High School

I had a good high school experience. I excelled in cheerleading and could have gone to the super bowl to perform in its halftime show. My secret was I had a big mirror at my house. I used to practice the cheers in front of the mirror. I played the clarinet in the band from 4th grade thru 11th grade, played soccer, and was on the bowling league. I was nominated for prom queen, homecoming queen and was rewarded with "the one with the most school spirit" award. Well, it made my head big and that was my first mistake.

The bible says, "Pride goes before destruction, and a haughty spirit before a fall." My first boyfriend Tom once told me, "the higher you go, the harder you fall." It is true.

College

After high school I decided to go to Drexel University for Computer Engineering. My mom inspired me to go into the computer field. She is smart. I was curious about the word 'engineering'. I didn't know what it meant. I knew it had to do with math and science. I was really good at math and science was interesting.

I cheated in College. My friend Peter helped me <u>a lot</u> with coding (C++ and Java). I still failed and had to take the night class. Luckily, that class really held your hand through it. I passed it and enjoyed the class. I believe the class was called Data Structures. Anyway, I could do all the other classes on my own but I really struggled with the computer languages.

My degree taught me two things. One, I can do almost anything if I put my mind to it. Two, it taught me that some people in your life don't care to see you succeed. While going to college and after I graduated, I would get little comments about my efforts to succeed. The comments confused me at first. Now that I am older I have a better understanding of it all.

I remember being at some family gathering. My aunt Lori asked me, "Are you happy?" I was naïve and didn't understand her intentions of the question. I think she was trying to plant a seed of doubt in my mind, which I believe is very evil to do to a young woman trying to accomplish something as big as computer engineering. After I graduated, I had a really good paying job at PPL. I was getting paid 47,000 a year. We had another family function. My aunt Lisa says, "I think people should do what makes them happy." As a family member, I was expecting a more supportive reaction. I was expecting a more encouraging response like, "hey, I am happy for you. That is Great!" My cousin Jennifer said, "You just did it because your mom made you do it." I have no idea where this comment came from but whatever. No one can make you take on the Computer Engineering Curriculum at Drexel University. It is either you sink or you swim. My sister in law Mary said, "I don't think her heart's in it." All of these opinions hurt me. As time went by, I learned from this experience. It taught me to say, "I am happy for you" to others. I stopped going to family functions.

While I was going to college, I lived with my boyfriend Tom. His mom owned the duplex. Tom hurt his knee and was prescribed Oxycotin. Poor Tom got addicted to the shit. He started to make money off of it too. I remember all this money laying on top of the dining room table. They stopped giving him Oxycotin and started to give him Methadone. He kept his methadone in the sock drawer. He caught me stealing his methadone. Why did he put it in the sock drawer? I open that drawer everyday.

If he didn't want me to touch it, why wouldn't he think of a better place to put it? It makes me wonder. Did he want me to get addicted? Some men will use drugs to gain control over a girl.

Tom came to sit in my physics lecture. I looked at him. He looked like he was struck with awe as he gazed at the mathematics.

In my ethics class, we had to do a presentation. When I began to talk, I looked at the class. I saw a lot of faces full of hate. I dropped all of my index cards and was not prepared enough to talk without them. My mind went blank. I stood in front of class for what felt like an hour.

It was also required we do a Senior Design Presentation. This time I was prepared. It is the sound of your voice that freaks you out when you speak in front of an audience. I recorded my voice reciting my part of the presentation and listened to myself as I drove to Drexel. As I did my part of the presentation, I remember the woman teacher smiling like she was very proud of me. When I first began to talk, my voice was shaky. I saw a lot of hateful faces again. When I went to use the electronic pointer, it did not work. So, I walked to the front of the room and used my arms and hands instead. I don't think they expected me to do that because their faces went from hate to shock.

I picked Drexel because it has a Co-op. My Co-op experience was at Sunoco Headquarters and the Sunoco Refineries. I worked in the Network Support group. I guess college wasn't a total waist of my time. I learned a lot at my co-op. I learned a lot of people in the computer field don't know what they are doing. The key is to act like you know. Sunoco taught me one valuable thing—the word 'redundancy'. Always have a plan B. On 9-11 I was at Sunoco Headquarters. I was watching it live. I caught it when the first building was smoking and the other building was untouched. I thought those people probably had a lot of pride working in the twin towers. I then thought, "what am I doing with my life?" My life consists of stress from trying to constantly stay on top of deadlines, papers, presentations, quizzes, homework, and classes. Life is so precious and I'm using most of it being stressed out.

In high school, I had stylish clothes, my hair was stylish, I wore makeup and even wore high heels. When I got to college, it seemed looking good didn't even matter anymore. <u>At all</u>. I lost all sense of fashion.

After I graduated, I was pretty burnt out. I needed a break so I did nothing for one year. Eventually my student loans kicked in. I needed money. I applied everywhere and anywhere. I jumped from one job to another for some reason: more money, temporary to permanent position, whatever the reason. I got tired of running around so I stayed at this one company called HAVCO. I worked in the kitchen there. My student loan payment was 600 a month, so all my money went to that.

PPL

I had a job at PPL. I drove an hour and a half to this place. I was getting paid 47,000 a year, but I was getting chest pains. The chest pains would last long. Not long, but long enough to scare the shit out of you. Working with a bunch of men, I felt stupid and unwanted. I felt like I didn't belong or wasn't good enough. I felt like I intruded the 'no girls allowed society'. In school, I was ignorant to the fact I was a girl in a male dominated field. It wasn't until after graduation it hit me that guys might possibly think 'what does this girl know?' It certainly doesn't help when you are pretty. Then people really think you are stupid. Did you ever notice girl's magazines are about makeup, jewelry, fashion, hair styles, and perfume. Guy's magazines have funny and interesting articles about different stuff. Don't get me wrong, being a girl can be fun at times, but reading about makeup is boring.

My time with Tom

Tom was my first boyfriend. We were together for 12 years. When I met him I was 15, and he was 17. He was a good guy. He resurrected. Metaphorically. Everyone called him a loser. Well, he ended up owning his own drywall business. Now he drives a bright red Toyota Tundra Truck. In the beginning of our relationship we experienced a lot of tragedy. His two childhood best friends died in a drunk driving accident. Tom's sister Dana was married to a man named Justice. Justice got into a really bad argument with his brother Ed. Justice ended up shooting Ed. Ed had a child. The way I look at it, a part of him still lives on.

One night I had a dream of a white door with gold plated numbers 54. Tom woke me up saying out loud, "what does the 54th time mean?" I told him that I was just dreaming about that number. I asked him, "Why do you ask that?" He said, "I don't know. I just blurted it out." I immediately felt overwhelmed with fear. Ever since then I had this thing for the number 54. I thought maybe it had some purpose in my life.

One day, I was walking in Penny Pack Park. I felt horrible for cutting off my friends. Two women jogged by me. As they passed the one said, "Friends are important but I can choose who they are." I stopped and looked down. 54 was spray painted on the cement trail. They could have been talking about anything, and they said it at the exact time they passed me.

I told this story to Stephanie who was my boss at Tuesday Morning. She showed me Psalm 54 in the bible. It is a psalm that asks god for protection from your enemies. I am glad she really listened to me. Most people don't listen.

I found another biblical scripture with the number 54. It is Isaiah 54. Part of the scripture states that god is our husband. I guess this particular scripture is for a woman, and god is a male.

I broke up with Tom over the phone in the office at Tuesday Morning. When I got off the phone, my co-worker told me the song "breaking up is hard to do" played when I was in the office. I said, "for real!" He put his hands in the air and said, "I swear."

My time in the mental institution

When I was about 27, I broke up with Tom and moved into my parent's house. It is really hard to have your own place and then have to move back into your parent's house. They thought I was acting weird so they forced me to go to a psychiatrist. My very first diagnosis was a nervous breakdown. The doctor put me on Ambilify and Respiradone. I was very angry at my parents for forcing me to go to a doctor. I really had no choice. It was I take the meds or I move out. Well, I let my parents have their way for a little while, and then I moved out. I moved into my second boyfriend Jacob's house. He lived with his dad, uncle and his uncle's girlfriend. When I moved out, I stopped taking my meds and had a psychotic episode. It is a horrible experience.

I have been institutionalized about 5 times. I have been in Lower Bucks Hospital, Fairmount, and Belmont. A woman in the institution told me that I should listen to music all the time. I took her advice. It's funny how you can learn the cleverest things in the weirdest places. You can learn anywhere you go even if it is McDonalds.

I was sitting next to a man in the TV room. He was preaching about god. I told him, "I asked god to make me an instrument of him, and he sent me here." I just started to cry. He told me that we all have to go through trials and tribulations. I think his name was Eric.

When I woke up from my sleep, I noticed a black man staring at me. He was sitting in the dining room. He wanted to buy me food. I think he bought me a cheese steak. He took his hat off. He told me he was hit in the head with a bat, and it showed. I believe he had a near death experience or something like it. He was telling me god is real.

When I was going through a psychotic phase, I always had a feeling the devil was coming for me. The weird thing about it was that a movie called, "Devil" was previewing on TV at the time of my sickness. What a coincidence! The day that movie was released to theaters was the date I thought the devil was coming to the institution.

There were very interesting people in the institution. My one roommate seemed really slow, but she played the piano very well in music class. There was this really big guy. He smelled really bad. He knew all the answers to the Jeopardy questions.

There was this one woman who scared me to death. I just got done taking my meds and I could feel them taking their effect. I heard her say, "Someone just took medication. I'm just waiting for it to kick in." She asked me the weirdest question, "Do you believe a person can be tortured without being touched?" They changed my room. She ended up being my roommate. I was petrified.

They changed my room again. I lay in my bed. I was praying to myself. "Our father who art in heaven hallow be thy name . . ." My room mate was praying the same exact thing at the same exact time. Only she was saying it out loud.

For some strange reason, I was afraid to get a shower.

I think the last time I was in the institution; I was in there for three months. I was convinced the devil was coming for me. The doctor would ask me if I seen the devil. I would reply no. He then would ask if I heard the devil's voice. I would reply no. The doctor decided to give me a CAT scan. The CAT scan was going to be done in another place so they put my arms and legs in restraints. I could hardly walk. When we got to the hospital, I sat in the waiting room. People were probably staring at me since I was restrained.

The medication made my legs shake. My legs shook so bad that it drove other people crazy. The medication also made my bladder weak. I would piss myself all the time.

Every morning a woman down the hall would scream at the top of her lungs. She would scream for quite a while.

I was afraid of the one room. It was only that one room. They ended up putting me in that room.

I wanted to cut my hair. They didn't give me the scissors, so I got pissed off and kicked the door. They restrained me. I remember the one guy pressed down on my bruise.

I was being transported to the hospital. As I lay there I could see a van behind us. There was a very creepy girl in the other van. She was snapping her head back and forth like she was keeping an eye on me and talking to someone sitting beside her. She was so creepy looking that I thought she was something evil and not of this world. The van followed for awhile but then eventually turned.

I'm lying in my bed at night. I heard someone scream so I ran to my door to see what was going on. When I came back into my room, my roommate was lying in her bed with the sheet all the way over her head. She was in a strange position. She looked like a dead body. I felt overwhelmed with fear when I saw her like that. I thought that the scream was a distraction to get me to look away from her. I felt like something was in the room and it wasn't good. My sister in law, Mary, said that maybe the scream was a good distraction. It made me leave the room.

I couldn't have the lights off. I was afraid of the dark.

At Lower Bucks Hospital, my very first mental institution, I colored a lot. I helped a man by writing letters for him. The letters were for his wife or girlfriend. He loved the Rolling Stones. It was a weird coincidence that my roommate had the same exact birthday as my boyfriend Jacob. April 18th. I made her a homemade card by cutting out pictures out of a magazine.

Coming up the steps from a cigarette break, I put a girl in a head lock. I also grabbed a guy's walkman out of his hands and threw it against the ground as hard as I could.

Waiting in line for medication, I pulled down the pants of the guy standing in front of me.

There was a colossal snowman made of colored paper taped to the wall. I kept taking its buttons off and putting them where his private parts would be. I got in trouble and two guards carried me to a solitary room. One guy had my legs. The other guy had my arms. When I got to the room, I just laid there on the cold cement floor. Hopeless. The monitor said, "Come on, get up, please." From the tone of his voice, he sounded like he felt bad for me.

We had music class. The intern's voice made me cry. Her voice was beautiful.

On cigarette break, I was sitting on the bench. I was staring at a star. There was a container to put your cigarette butts into. It was full of sand and was really heavy. It held the door opened. I remembered the one guy picked it up, probably about 2 inches off the floor, and slammed it back on the ground. He did it a couple of times. I didn't see him do it but I heard it. Another guy asks him, "Is it moving?" The guy who was playing with the cigarette butt container said, "Yeah." The star I was staring at started to move like it was an airplane.

I would be so scared at night that I would stay up all night and sleep during the day.

The place that we had our cigarette break had a busy road near it. I remember one night. I saw this guy riding on a motorcycle. Now I only saw him for a second. He didn't look like a usual person. The motorcycle was really big and black. The rider was also in all black. The only way to describe it was that it looked like a motorist from the depths of hell. When I seen him/it I immediately thought it was of an evil nature. Right after it passed by, the one guy said to the other guy, "that was my people." The other guy replied with a smirk as if he was saying, "No, that was my people."

I was so bad psychologically that I thought the people in my life were dead. When they came to visit me, I thought that it wasn't really them. They were imposters. I thought that they just looked like the people I loved. When I sat in the waiting room with them, I felt like I was sitting with an evil spirit who took the form of a family member. When Jacob came to visit me, I started to cry. I said, "It isn't him."

Sometimes when faced with extreme challenges, it gives you a chance to discover yourself and how strong you really can be. Being so afraid of the devil, my mind started to cope. I would think, "I am absolute power. God made me. I was made to overthrow the devil. To lure him in, to trick him." This made me feel better.

However, there were always those moments when I was afraid. I read in the bible. I believe in the Proverbs. Man should wait for god when faced with evil. That only god can defeat evil.

Me, Dottie, and another girl shared a room. One night the girl had the worst smelling gas. It was so bad Dottie and I had to complain to the staff. They knew about her gas and sympathized. They came in our room and sprayed it down with air freshener. That girl was totally crazy and she was getting released pretty early, which I didn't understand. Then I thought maybe she was just so bad that they thought it wasn't possible to fix her.

I met Dottie at the mental institution. When I first met her she was in pretty bad shape. Now she is all better and let me tell you she is the most normal person I ever met. She is starting college in September and plans to become a scientist. I wish her the best of luck. She told me a ghost story and it made me quiver. She told me her grandmother's favorite show was recorded and no one watches that show. Her grandmother was the only one who watched that show. Her grandmother is dead.

Some psychotic experiences

One time I was having a really bad psychotic episode. I was running in the middle of the street. My boyfriend Jacob was trying to push me out of the street. He yelled, "Get out of the street!" He called my sister. It took three people to hold me down until the cops came. I am only 130 pounds and 5' 4". The cops put me in the paddy wagon. It was pitch black. I was petrified.

It was New Years Eve. I was at Jacob's. He went to his friend's house. He asked me if I wanted to go but I said no. I recently got out of Fairmount. It is a mental institution. When I was released, I did not continue my meds. I went through a terrible psychotic episode. All night I sat by the front door. I thought my boyfriend was getting tortured in hell. It made me so sad that I put a knife to my chest. I thought if I killed myself I would go to hell too, but I was too afraid to go to hell.

When I lived with my mom and dad, I walked outside in my underwear, bra, and coat. Supposedly, I made a sandwich for one of my buddies chilling in the woods (my back yard). I got the coat at Tuesday Morning when I worked there. When it first got there, I thought to myself, "Damn, that is one ugly coat." I ended up buying it. It was the last one like it (color wise). The coat was reversible. It had fake fur on one side and suede on the other side. I would wear it with the fur on the inside. It came down to my knees. The suede was black. The fur looked like Tai Lung's fur on Kung Fu Panda. Tai Lung is Chinese for great dragon. The character is a snow leopard.

One time I was flipping out so bad the guards put me in restraints. I thought my boyfriend was in hell and he was being tortured. I screamed, "I want it as bad as him!" They tried to calm me down. They said, "Okay baby." They said it so gently like they felt so bad for me.

I felt like I was getting sick (mentally) so I walked myself to Friends. Friends is a mental institution. On the way, I stopped and sat on a bench. Across the street, there was an apartment complex. There was a sign hanging up. It said, "You can move here." Something made me get up off the bench and rip down the sign. I continued to walk to Friends with the sign in my hand. All I had to do was walk across the Roosevelt Blvd and I was at Friends. I walked against traffic. The cars swerved out of my way. I still had the sign in my hand. The sign said, "You can *move* here."

I put a knife to my chest and heard a room full of laughter.

Sitting in Jacob's room, the basement, I heard bells jingling upstairs. I said to myself, "what is that? What is up there?" I was very scared. I had a feeling it wasn't something good. It was like it wanted me to come upstairs and see what it was.

Living with Mom and Dad

When I lived with my mom and dad, I took a lot of walks. They would get angry because I would walk late in the night sometimes. One night I was walking and I asked god to make me pure. After I said that it rained. It only rained for 10 seconds. I don't know exactly how long it rained but it was only for a short time.

My mother had a dream. It was actually a nightmare. She believes she's psychic. She saw me standing over her. She said it scared the shit out of her. My parents locked their bedroom door when they went to sleep. That really hurt my feelings.

I was lonely when I was living with my mom and dad, so I drank a lot. I found whiskey and got drunk most of the time. My parents didn't know I was drinking. After I was put on meds, I still continued to drink. Well, that was a bad idea. I got into a really big fight with them one day. It was so bad that my father was holding me down on the couch until the cops arrived. Supposedly I said to my father, "I will cut your balls off." Until this day, I do not remember saying that. Let's just say, I was no longer allowed to live there anymore.

The time I almost died

Jacob and I were sitting in his room smoking weed. His room was in the basement. The kitchen was right at the top of the steps. I heard someone in the kitchen. I told Jacob that I thought the devil was in the kitchen. I never really had thoughts like this until after I was put on meds. He told me that it was either his uncle or his dad or his uncle's girlfriend in the kitchen. After awhile we got hungry and decided to see what there was to eat. There was a bucket of roast beef slices. I ate a piece of roast beef. It was the kind of roast beef meat that is on a hot roast beef sandwich. I started choking and gasping for air. It is a horrible feeling. Jacob's uncle Oliver was trying to do the Heimlich maneuver on me, but it didn't work. After awhile my knees buckled. Jacob's dad, John, was upstairs sleeping. I was almost dead so Oliver called for John. Out of no where, Jacob shoved his finger down my throat. I gagged and the meat finally came up.

Living with My sister

Tonya is my brother Mark's first wife. I have two brothers by the way. They are both older than me. Their names are Mark and Luke. Mark is the oldest. He got married twice. I don't talk to Mark that much. I do talk to Luke. Tonya is technically not my sister, but she was there when everyone else turned their back on me. In her household, there is her mother (a.k.a. mum mum or Karen), her husband, her three kids (Sarah, Joe, and Debbie), Sam (family friend), me, and Bubba (the family dog). That's a lot of people isn't it? When I lived there, I admit I was extremely lazy. I would just sit on the couch all day long and listen to my walkman everyday. Sometimes I would read the dictionary. I wanted to learn big words. People take you seriously when you speak eloquently. What I thought was interesting was 'how' they described the big word using a bunch of small words.

I knew I should clean the house but I just couldn't bring myself to do it. I felt like a piece of shit. I may have been suffering from depression. After all, my parents sold my car. I haven't had a job for awhile because I was waiting for Social Security Benefits to kick in.

I remember going into the Social Security Office with Tonya. The guy asked Tonya "Is she capable of handling her money?" Instead of saying yes, Tonya said some other bullshit. I cried. I got a form from him in front of Tonya. The form was for my doctor to fill out. If filled out correctly, it states that I am capable of handling my money. I got the form filled out and mailed it in. Tonya was mad at me for getting it filled out without telling her. She was there when I asked for the form. She was there when the guy gave it to me. So the way I look at it, she was just mad she couldn't have control of my money. I don't know why she thought I owed her. I gave her my welfare card for as long as I was at her house. That was 200 dollars every month in food stamps and 200 dollars every month in cash.

Chaos during my early months of pregnancy

My social security benefits were about to kick in. I waited for them for about 2 years. I was expecting 25,000. That money is based on my work history. I suspected my sister, Tonya, was after my money, but I did not say anything to her until one day. She asked me if I could buy her a computer. For some reason I just couldn't hold in my feelings anymore. I told her that the money I am getting is going to be for the baby's needs. We argued. She threatened me by saying, "I'm calling SSI tomorrow." I said, "Tonya, I can change my overseer." In special cases, people who receive SSI/SSD need someone to control their money. That person is called the overseer. At this point, I had enough, and I snapped. I said, "I don't need SSI. I have a degree." I pushed the dining room chair into the dining room table. She got up, walked toward me, and punched me in the face. I screamed, "You think I'm afraid of you because you're bigger than me!" Tonya's mother, mum mum, yelled, "She's pregnant!" We stopped fighting. I called Richard, my baby's father. He is half white and half black. He had his friend Charles pick me up. Richard was in Florida. He wanted to go to college.

Charles drove me to his house. Richard's mother and sister picked me up from there. I moved into their home. I thought that I was in the clear, but I wasn't. I became the topic of conversation. My family was telling everyone I was crazy, so people that didn't know me didn't really know how to take me. They were confused. It was so bad that Richard called me one night and asked me where I was the other night. I said, "What night are you talking about?" He told me that someone told him that I was out all night and didn't come home until early in the morning. I knew at that moment people were really going to extremes to ruin my life. People are so manipulative. It's so sad. I feel so sorry for them. I didn't trust anyone. Richard told me that he has a lot of family in Philly and that I was being watched.

Meanwhile, Sam asked Tonya, "What would you have done if you hurt her?" Tonya said, "I would have told the cops she's schizophrenic and I was defending myself." If Tonya threw the first punch, how can that be true? It was then I knew she was crazy.

When I lived with Richard's mom, life wasn't any easier. Richard's mother really came down on me—like a ton of bricks. She would say all sorts of negative comments like, "You can't even take care of yourself. Your parents didn't teach you anything about life. You have no friends and that's not how a 30 year old life should be. I'm afraid you are going to drop the baby if you flip out." She told me a story about a woman who had bipolar. The woman drowned her babies in the tub. Part of me admired the fact she wasn't holding back. In other words, she didn't talk behind my back. She told me to my face. I didn't really know what to say back, so I told her not to worry. Everything will be okay.

The day before father's day I called my dad's cell. He didn't pick up. My mother ended up calling me back. I asked her to put dad on the phone. I could hear his voice in the background. She told me he was in the bathroom. I said, "He doesn't want to talk to me?" She said, "No." I cried.

Because of all the stress, I couldn't eat. I had to force myself to eat. Even though my life was spinning out of control, all I could do was thank god for my sanity. There is nothing worse than a psychotic episode.

I sat on the couch. A commercial was on TV. They were advertising gym equipment. I thought to myself, "Protect me from my enemies. They are praying for my downfall. I am scared." At that exact moment, the lady on TV said, "Don't be afraid". She said a few words after she said don't be afraid. I don't recall what they were. All I know is she said 'don't be afraid' right as I was thinking, "I am scared."

On top of it all, my doctor calls me and tells me I have a urinary track infection.

Tyler is my friend. I knew him way before I knew Richard. Tyler is also Richard's cousin. Tyler took me to the bank, my doctors, and Rite Aid. I told Richard's mom I wouldn't be long, but when I came back the door was locked.

I sat at Burger King with Irene, Richard's sister. I told her, "I don't know if I can take care of a baby financially." She told me that I can do it. She gave me a hug. Irene said, "Maybe you should go to church." We laughed.

My friend Sam taught me to never tell people what you are planning to do. He said, "It is better to just do it." So as I searched for an apartment, I didn't tell anyone. Sam was the only one who knew.

On the day I moved into my very first apartment, Tyler called me. He said his car battery died. He was my ride to the apartment! My heart dropped. Sam was working so he couldn't take me. I found Mike's number and called him. Mike is my case worker. Mike answered and I was surprised. Tyler ended up getting a jump. He got me to the apartment on time.

Shortly after I got to the apartment, Mike stopped over. We went to the food store. I got food, one pan, one pot, silverware, dish drain, etc.

The same day I moved into my apartment, Richard broke up with me. He thought I was having sex for money and Sam was my pimp. Richard screamed, "Don't pull the wool over my eyes! I am smart. You talk about Sam like he is great. What am I? Chop Suey!" So I called Tyler. I cried to him. Tyler said, "You're not going to do anything stupid are you?"

I found out Richard cheated on me with a girl he drove from Virginia to North Carolina. I went through so much. When he told me he cheated it didn't hurt.

Only three people know where my apartment is. Tyler, Mike, and Sam.

My credit was only a 59. Wayne, my landlord, let me slide. I was supposed to have at least a 60.

When I moved in my apartment, Sam moved in too. I don't know why he did this. I did not ask him to move in with me so why would he assume it was okay? Sam put his weed stash into my tote. I yelled at him and told him to put it with his shit. One night we were lying on the floor. There was a bunch of stuff in the middle of us: cigarettes, ashtray, his phone, etc. He started to move the stuff out of the way. I thought to myself, "What the hell is he doing?" He laid closer to me. I don't know what he was trying to do, but I shoved him away. After everything I just went through, this was the last thing I wanted to deal with. When we lived at my sisters, I remember sitting next to him on the couch. He moved closer to me. He was getting close to my ear with his mouth. I don't know what he wanted to do but I moved away. That was one time that I rejected his advancements. Another time I rejected him was in my sister's kitchen. He wrapped his arms around me from behind as I was trying to put the food away. I told him to fall back. If I rejected him twice already, why is he still trying to get close to me? This annoyed me very much.

On another day, Sam said, "We're going to write this book." I usually don't do this but I reacted quickly and said, "What do you mean we?" It made me think, "Why did he say that. What are his intentions? Does he

31

want me to split the profits?" He said, "You will write the book, and I will help you publish it." I said, "I will write the book, and I will publish it." I immediately started to ask Sam about the apartment he put a down payment on. Supposedly, Sam put a down payment on an apartment, but he couldn't move into it just yet. It needed to be renovated or something. It was at this moment I started to lose trust in Sam. I read a book called "The Everything Birthday Personology Book." The book had all the days of the year. I looked up March 2, which is my birthday. It said, "Opportunists see your abilities and hope to take advantage of them, without giving you any credit."

Journal Entries

There is a church right around the corner of my apartment complex! I am so happy about that. This church does not pass the money hat! There is a box where you can give donations. They have bible study every Wednesday. I met a woman named Katana at church. She showed me her husband. She said she is a cougar, since he is much younger than her. I laughed. She told me she was happy she found him. I told her I'm happy for her. I told her it is hard to find a good man. I am single and I kind of like it.

I ordered 5 CDs from Best Buy. I got 20th Century Masters: Millennium Collection (Remastered)—Sublime, Narrow Stairs—Death Cab for Cutie, Wedding Crashers [ECD]—Enhanced Original Soundtrack, Greatest Hits: Every Mile a Memory—Dierks Bentley, Donuts—J. Dilla, The Score—Fugees.

Artist	Track #	Name of song	CD #
Death cab for cutie	4	Cath	
	5	Talking Bird	
	11	The ice is getting thinner.	
Dierks Bentley	4	Come a Little Closer	
J.Dilla	6	Stop	
	10	Time: the Donut of the Heart	
	16	One Eleven	
	27	U-love	
	29	Bye	
	30	Last donut of the night	
Babyface tender lover	11	where will you go	
Sade lovers rock	1	By your side	
Dave Matthews Band the complete weekend at Red Rocks	4, 8		CD 7
	9		CD 4
Gorillaz demon days	6	Feel good inc.	

Wedding Crashers: the song I was searching for wasn't one of the songs on the CD.

UPS cannot get into our complex since it is locked. You need a key to get into the complex and another key for your apartment. So I waited outside for my CDs to be delivered since I already missed the UPS truck's first attempt. As I sat there, I thought to myself. My biological mom gave me up. My parents forced me on meds and then kicked me out of the house. My sister punched me and kicked me out. I was in and out of mental institutions. I am in 55,000 dollars of student loan debt, and I am only 30. I waited from 10:30 to 1:30 for UPS to arrive.

I called Creekside Motors about a black 95 Honda Accord. It is a stick shift so I got to have it. When you park a stick shift, you must put the emergency brake up. Otherwise, the car could roll. My car rolled down the street into someone else's car a long time ago when I had my first car. Tom taught me how to drive a stick shift. He gave me two cars.

I walked all over for a map of Philadelphia. I wanted a map in case I get lost driving. I walked to WAWA, Rite Aid, 3 gas stations, library, Shoprite, and Walgreens. 7-eleven ended up having the map.

I set myself up with car insurance. I chose Geico. I only had to pay 279 for 6 months!

I went to church. When it was over I ran out of there so fast. After all the bullshit I've been through I wasn't interested in meeting anyone. I remember a young black boy in front of me at church. He was sitting by himself. I was really proud of him.

I plan to get my tubes tied after I give birth to this baby. If I really am crazy I don't want to pass it down to my children. It isn't fun. I also decided that I don't want to get married nor do I want to live with anyone.

I bought long dresses and posters for my apartment. One poster is a white tiger lying in the snow. Another one is a women walking off a cliff. The cliff is about a foot or two above the ocean. She is blindfolded. If she makes one more step she will fall into the water, but a giant transparent hand is waiting to catch her. I have a painting of a man break dancing and he is surrounded by people. They all look surprised. Another poster is two giraffes showing affection by resting each other's heads on the other. Marilyn Monroe laying on a weight bench lifting weights is another poster on my apartment wall. All the posters were from South Street. The break dancer was from Target. I filled my window sill with a variety of seashells. I have two windows in my living room so I bought stained glass art to hang in my windows. One is a girl riding on a Pegasus. The other is a mermaid. There are three hooks on my ceiling right in front of the windows. I bought fish line and hung a fairy. She is blowing a kiss. Also hanging from the ceiling is a little boy with wings. He is standing on a cloud and playing a viola. An angel sitting on a crescent moon hangs from the ceiling in my apartment. The electricity has been on for a month now.

Pastor Albert's wife, Jasmine, taught me something at church. I told her I want to read the bible but I just don't understand it. She told me to read the Proverbs. So if you want to read the bible, but don't understand it, read the Proverbs.

I bought a queen sized airbed. It cost 100.00. It is double high and has a built in pump. I bought 2 fold up chairs (5.88 a piece), and 2 fold out tables (8.99 a piece). I got corn rolls and long red hair extensions. I loved it, but it made my head itch like crazy.

I went to Drexel and got my degree back. I had to pay for it. I threw the original one in the street when I was sick (mentally).

In college, I learned hardcore mathematics. For instance, physics class. It makes me wonder. Between math and faith, there is so much to the world that we don't see, know or understand. There is so much more above and beyond. It is quite mind blowing.

I bought nail polish today. It is a metallic bronze. It's really pretty. I like it a lot. The name of the color is "it's possible." Out of all the colors I could have chosen, I chose the one that says, "It's possible."

Today I bought a 4 panel oriental room divider. I got a fly catcher to hang on my ceiling. It looks like 2 flies are dead on it. Gross!

I have a bonsai tree. I put a fake blue bird on the edge of the pot. Every morning when I wake up I water the Bonsai tree and take my prenatal vitamin. I would be so upset if my bonsai tree died. I never had to take care of a plant before. My bonsai tree is so beautiful, so tranquil.

I bought 3 movies by Hayao Miyazaki. I can describe his movies with one word. Imagination. I figured it will be good for my kid. I think it was Albert Einstein who said imagination is more important than knowledge.

I started playing the power ball every Wednesday and Saturday. I plan to play the same six numbers for the rest of my life. I figure it just may come out. If I win I will give some to my brother so he can open his own auto repair shop.

I tried hanging out with someone from my apartment complex, but he liked me and started to kiss me all over. I had to ask him to leave. Guys are more fun to hang out with until they start trying to be more than friends.

Instead of buying cable, I borrow movies from the library. You are allowed to borrow up to 10 DVDs a day.

I went to Wells Fargo to withdrawal 5000 dollars. I wanted to put it on my Great Lakes student loan. They ended up shorting me 100 dollars. They didn't believe me when I complained about it. They said that two people counted the money. I told them that I didn't care if two people counted the money. My money was short! Later they called me to notify me that they found the 100 dollars on the floor. Always count your money before you leave the bank.

Sam moved out around late July 2011. Before he left he told me that his check would be coming to my address. I checked the mailbox but the check wasn't there. Sam would call me but I didn't pick up. I changed my phone number.

Today is Saturday, July 30, 2011. I picked up two Mexicans from Home Depot. I paid them to help me get a crib from Walmart to my apartment.

I sat in the hot sun waiting for the damn UPS truck to arrive. I even rescheduled my doctor's appointment. I was waiting for my degree. I went through hell to get that degree. I want it. I had my Gregory Isaacs (reggae) CD, my Barrington Levy CD (reggae), and my Mazzy Star CD. I had the bible with me. I sat on my fold out chair. I started to read the Psalms starting with the last one. Psalm 150. A girl passing by gave me a cold bottle of water! I thought that was so nice. It made me happy. A guy who lives in my apartment complex came out and we chatted. His name was Pat. He was a roofer and has eleven children. He gave me a bunch of DVDs to watch.

I spent 70 bucks on a converter box and antenna. I got it at Barracks Trading Post on Street Road.

I read all the Psalms. It took me about 6 hours. While I read them I wrote down 7 sentences that describe god. I plan to give the notes to Joe. A while back he asked, "Who is god?" No one answered him. The seven things I wrote down were:

1. God is the Judge
2. Power belongs to god
3. whenever you are afraid, trust in god
4. god will be our guide
5. he is a great king over all the
6. earth the lord crushes the wicked
7. god is love

Notes 1-5 I got from reading the Psalms. As I was writing down the description of god for Joe, I had Gangs of New York playing on my DVD Player. Leonardo Dicaprio said, "The lord crushes the wicked." Since this is true, I included it.

I think Leonardo Dicaprio is handsome. He is an awesome actor. He got his name because his mom was looking at a Leonardo da Vinci painting when he first kicked in her womb. I liked Jonny Depp in the tourist. I think Angelina Jolie is really good. I liked Brad Pitt in 12 monkeys and Snatch. I liked Uma Thurman in Kill Bill. I like the part when she is surrounded by her enemies and she starts break dancing with swords in her hands.

Quentin Tarantino is smart. I have Kill Bill volume 2. I got it for free. When I bought the TV, I got the movie.

I do not find myself worthy enough to preach about god, and I do not wish to push my beliefs unto others. However, Joe did ask this question. To me this is special and I find it important to answer him. It is said, "If you seek him, you shall find him." After I gave Joe the note, I told him that if he didn't want to read it he can just throw it away. That is his choice. I think he is about 12 or 13 so he just might throw it away but I hope he reads it just one more time. I tried to make the words simple for him to understand but I think he still struggled to really comprehend. After all we are talking about a supernatural force that is not spoken of regularly. I am glad people don't talk about god, because I do not find anyone who is worthy enough to portray him/herself as a servant of god. We are all sinners and hypocrites. To display oneself as a celestial being could very well be an abomination to the lord. In other words, when you meet someone and they seem good because they speak of god. It does not necessarily mean they are righteous. I think it is better to be looked at as neutral, lost, or crazy keeping in mind that you know who you are. On the other hand I am grateful for my church because it is a place where I can learn the writings of the bible. I cannot understand it on my own. The knowledge is way too deep. It is a fanciful enigma.

The day I gave Joe the note I had to knock on the door since the phone line was busy. I got to see Bubba so I am thankful for that. Bubba is a boxer. He looks mixed with pit bull. He is so beautiful. I love him. My eyes water as I write this. When I lived at Tonya's Bubba used to sleep with me on the couch.

I watched my childhood dog die. It broke me into a million pieces. It ripped my heart apart. Her name was Sybil. She was a mutt. She was part German Shepard. She had diabetes. We left her with a veterinarian so we could go to my cousins wedding. I think it was in New York. When we got back she was all messed up. Her paws were bloody like she was desperately trying to escape from her cage. Her eyes were filled with puss. I ran back to the veterinarian and asked him, "What did you do to my dog!" He said, "I think she wasn't used to being left in a kettle and she wouldn't eat." It hurts to think she thought we left her. I used to play hide and seek with her. My father would cover her eyes while I hid. She would look for me. If she didn't find me after awhile she would start to cry. When I played my clarinet she would sit beside me and howl. I thought that it hurt her ears. If it hurt her ears she would not have sat next to me. She probably would have left the room. After she died there was nothing to greet me when I got home from school. If I could turn back time, I would have stayed home with my dog rather than go to that wedding. It is horrible to see something/someone you love die right in front of your eyes and not be able to do a damn thing to help them. I think she went through a diabetic shock.

I talked to a girl named Candy. She is from my apartment complex. She just had a baby. She told me about gripe water by tummy time. She said that babies cry because of gas, and this will help them with that. It was very useful information! I was grateful for it.

I am thinking about making a portfolio and becoming a model. I figure it's worth a shot since I am in 50,000 of student loan debt. I have an appointment with John Robert Powers tomorrow. Being pretty can be a curse. Girls hate you and you can't be friends with guys because they always try to make things sexual.

I found a place that sells baby clothes for 50 cents! Knowledge is a beautiful thing.

I went to the library to get model agency numbers. While waiting for a PC I was interested in a couple of the astrology books. I am a Pisces. Erykah Badu is too. My birthday is March 2. I looked up my birthday in a book called, "The Everything Birthday Personology Book." It said, "There is little room in your life for rude, inconsiderate, or willfully ignorant people. That outlook developed from rather turbulent personal experiences, but it serves you well nonetheless." In an astrology book called, "Your Story in the Stars." I learned that Albert

Einstein was a Pisces. It stated, "Your symbol is two fish, swimming in opposite directions. The fact that the fish aren't moving in the same direction represents the inner struggle you sometimes experience. When your heart wants to go one way and your head demands to go in another direction." This can describe the way I feel about spending 1000 towards Sarah's EMT School. In another book of astrology I learned that Pisces are mutable. Michelangelo is Pisces. It stated, "Neptune, planet of inspiration and imagination, is your ruler. It is also the planet of illusion." The name of this book is, "Your Stars at Work." Pisces is the most unworldly and sensitive of all the signs.

People remind me of a horse pulling a carriage in center city. Those horses do not seem happy. When I see a wild horse running free, it is so beautiful to me because the horse looks happy. I want to be like the wild horse.

I called Caesar Elite, model agency. They said they can do a portfolio for 96 dollars but I have to go to the website to describe the environment I want my portfolio to take place. I thought about it and this is what I plan to write, "I want it to be pure—like in a park/forest or something. I want it to be calm, serene. I do not wish to smile. I want to show poise, boldness. I want to profuse a strong vigor but I do not want to disregard modesty and tranquility. Like a white tiger who just got done eating. The white tiger is satisfied and does not desire to kill in this moment. Also, I lack confidence when it comes to posing. I am hoping for a little bit of training in the process."

My car radio was stolen out of my car. Luckily they didn't break my window. I am the ninth car they did it too. I had some extra cash and got a new one from Barracks. I paid 45 for the radio and 35 for installation. My new car radio has a removable face plate. Hopefully that will deter them the next time. My neighbor across the hall told me someone broke into his apartment last November and stole all his kid's Christmas gifts. I called ADT to get set up with an alarm system.

I spoke to a guy from my apartment complex. He has only been in America for a year. He is from Africa. His name is William. He told me about Africa. He taught me about Cameroon. It is a country in Africa. In Cameroon there are two cities named Douala and Yaounde. In these cities you can get a place with 3 bedrooms, living room, kitchen for about 80/month. A taxi is about 40 cents. You can also get a place in center city for 200/month. A house is only 40,000. I found this information very interesting.

I asked my neighbor how much she spent on baby wipes a month. She said she uses about 2 packs a week. Wipes are about 2 dollars a pack. This comes out to be 16 dollars a month. She gets Wick and told me that they give about 32 jars of food a month. Her baby eats about 6 jars a day. One jar of food is about 1.19. That calculates to 178 dollars a month. Someone at church told me I can buy cheap diapers on Amazon.com.

I found this place that sells baby stuff. I got 5 things and spent only 100 dollars. I got a swing, high chair, walker, car seat, and stroller.

I asked Mike to look into getting me subsidized daycare.

If I have a boy I am going to make him take break dancing classes. I won't tell anyone, I'll let it be his little surprise.

Today is August 6, 2011. I woke up, vacuumed, cleaned the bathroom, and watered my bonsai tree. I got a shower. I put on my 16.99 bracelet, my seashell necklace, my silver dangly clip on earrings, and my red lipstick. I wore a long dress and flip flops. I didn't do anything to my hair. I put lotion on my legs, arms, face, and feet. I drove to John Robert Powers. It is a modeling agency. I met a man by the name of Henry Ross. Everyone called him Ross. He told me that I need training and it would cost 800 dollars. It is a 10 week course. It will be 60 dollars a week and a 200 deposit. Henry Ross is a very cool man. I like him. This particular agency has been around since 1923. It is the oldest and largest school and agency in the Delaware Valley. Marilyn Monroe was one of the famous Powers people. I cannot pursue this because of two reasons. I will be getting nice and plump in the next few months. Two, I don't have the money. Ross told me to put 10 dollars a week away until I get enough money.

There was a sign outside across the street from the agency. Psychic readings 10.00. She had said some really bad things. She said since I was a baby I have been cursed. I carry negative energy and bad luck. She said she is going to burn 9 candles for me. I guess burning 9 candles is a spiritual ritual.

I got Chinese food. My fortune cookie said, "Good things are being said about you."

August 9, 2011: I took William to Target so he could get the double high queen sized airbed. I think he paid 89.99 for it. I paid 100.00. Mike came over. I told him I can't model because I don't have 800 and I am pregnant. He told me he had a friend who models. She modeled while she was pregnant, and she didn't have to pay 800 dollars. I went to the library to look up self publishing. I applied for a free publishing guide on two different websites. Both companies contacted me via phone. We discussed price. If I get a job now, I can get the book published in about 2 months. I am finally sitting on my brand new sofa. The sofa is sexy but classy. It is cream and leather. Tyler came over. He said, "I'm happy for you." That meant a lot to me.

August 10, 2011: Today I made a police report for my stolen car radio. I called the National Guard to discuss their Student Loan Repayment Program. They pay up to 50,000. They told me I have to join the National Guard. I would but I am pregnant. I guess I'm stuck with the 50,000 student loan debt. I took a trip to that special place on Rising Sun. I bought 12 baby outfits for 5.00! I bought a stroller for 30. The stroller I bought before isn't good for a newborn. A newborn needs to lie down in a stroller. I went to the welfare office to apply for help with health insurance. The health insurance I receive from SSD does not cover prescription costs. Today, I also applied for CAP. CAP is a program for low income households. With CAP, your electricity bill is lower. I set an appointment with WIC.

August 11, 2011: Sarah and I went to the EMT school so she could take the test. She did not take the test because she has a misdemeanor on her record, so we went downtown to the courthouse to see if we could get her record expunged. They told her that she needed to fill something out on the computer, print it out and come back with a 15 dollar money order. We stopped to get something to eat at Magiannos. I spent 13 bucks on a dish and only got 3 scallops! Parking was 20. Then we went to the library on Cottman, but it was closing. We went to the library on Castor. The computers were not allowing her to do what she needed to do. The librarian was nice enough to let Sarah use her computer. Sarah picked up two movies at the library. We went to my apartment and chilled. We ended up going to Blockbuster and getting the movie, "The Rite." It is pretty scary. It is about the devil.

I took some pictures of my apartment and sent them to Richard. He replied, "Your place is nice."

August 17, 2011: It's a boy! I am naming him after his father. I talked to Richard via text messaging. That was nice.

I decided to go food shopping. As I drove to the store, I heard a strange sound. It sounded like I drove something over so I stopped the car and looked under my car. Nothing was there. As I went to get back into the car a man stopped me. He said, "Your wheel is about to fall off." Lucky for me he was a mechanic and I was right out front of a mechanic shop! My wheel could have fell off while I was driving on I-95 on my way to my pastor's retirement party which was later on that day!

I threw in a load of clothes because I wanted my nude colored bra. After I washed the clothes I noticed the bra was missing. It is possible that someone stole it. However what would be the chances of them stealing the only item I was looking for?

I ran into my first boyfriend Tom on the Roosevelt Boulevard. He is married now and I am pregnant. It is such a shame because I would get back with him in a heartbeat. He was my best boyfriend. I left him for Jacob. When I was with Jacob I was in and out of the mental institution. Ultimately I want Tom to be happy. If he is happy with his wife I want him to stay with her.

Surprise!

1. At the Fairmount Mental institution, we were allowed to go to the gymnasium once in a while. When we went I would throw the football with a friend. One of the guards said, "Why don't you play basketball?" I said, "I don't know how." Later I tried to play basketball. For some strange reason I was standing and waiting at a certain spot on the court. Imagine you are the basketball net. In front of you in the distance is the other basketball net. I would be standing on your left hand side. That is where I was standing on the court all the way in the corner. For some reason someone threw the ball to me. Like an Asian girl in that point of the court would actually get the ball in. I did get it in. I remember playing basketball with Tyler and Sarah a long time ago. I remember saying, "I want to get it in from here." I would stand at the corners on each side of the basketball net. It's a hard shot.

2. We played softball in recess in high school. My team already had two outs, and I was up to bat. The gym teacher pitched the ball. I swung as hard as I could. Strike one. Someone on my team screamed, "This ball is going over there!" As he says this he points to the outfield. The

gym teacher pitches the ball again. Strike two. Now it is two outs and two strikes. This is it. Do or Die. The group of girls around first base started to move close to one another and started talking. This time when he pitched it, I could see the ball as it was coming to me. When I swung this time it went right towards the girls talking around first base. I started to run as fast as I could. As I ran to first base, the girl in the outfield was running to the ball. Her friends yelled to her, "Hurry!" I was safe. Recess was over soon after that.

When I first moved to Croydon (I was in 4th grade), I had a lot of boys on my street. I played a lot of waffle ball.

3. When I lived with mom and dad, I would use the swimming pool a lot. We had a basketball net for the pool. I would shoot the ball a lot.

My brother had a barbecue at my parent's house. All his friends were in the yard. I decided to go into the pool. I started to shoot the basketballs. We had 5 or 6. I was getting all of them in. I am not that good. It was strange. I remember my brother Luke and my dad walked by and smiled at me. They looked like they were proud of me.

4. Tom's dad was an extremely clean person. He loved music. Tom, his dad, and me went to AC. On the ride home the DJ was cutting it up. I don't remember the radio station or the name of the artist but the name of the song that was playing was called "Fools Paradise". I sang

this one part of the song. I remember that when I sang, it was so loud that Tom jumped out of his seat because it scared him. His dad looked in the rearview mirror and his face was awestruck. The song starts out like this:

> *I'm taking out this time . . . .*
> *To give you a piece of my mind . . . .*

Memories

My tattoo

Tom had a white pit-bull. We named him Blanco. It means white in Spanish. Blanco had two black spots on his body. He had a black spot on his backside near his tailbone. The other black spot was around his armpit of his front right leg. I loved this dog so much. I would come home from work and the first thing I do was get down on my knees and hug Blanco. Blanco would get on his hind legs and put his front legs on my shoulders. He would rest his head on mine like he really was hugging me.

When I was working at Tuesday Morning, Neil, a co-worker, gave me a bracelet. It had two emblems on it. It had a dragon and a phoenix. I never saw a phoenix before. I looked it up in the dictionary. I liked the meaning so I decided to get a tattoo of a phoenix. The guy drawing my tattoo asked me where I wanted it done. I lifted my right arm and showed him the location. It was the same spot Blanco had a black spot. After I showed him, he smirked. I thought, "Why is he smirking?" Now I know—It hurt so bad! I didn't consider the fact that the spot I chose is probably one of the most tender places to get a tattoo. The guy who gave me the tattoo is blind in one eye.

Ron at Dave and Busters

I took my nephew, Ron, to Dave and Busters for his birthday. I don't remember what age he was turning. He brought his friend. I don't remember his friend's name.

I remember Ron handing something to his friend and said, "Save this for a souvenir." I thought that was real cool. His friend was running around, and I was afraid I was going to lose him.

Ron approached this one game. It looked like a moderate sized circle in cased in plastic or something. Around the circumference of the circle there were numbers. Each number had its own space of the circle. Imagine a pie with many slices. Each slice has a number. I don't remember how many numbers, but let's just use 1000 as an example. The rules of this game were to press the button when the light shined on the number 1000. Now the light moves extremely fast around the circle. The light shines on each number for only an instant. Ron played. The light twinkled around the circle. Round and Round. Ron pounded on the button and it stopped on 1000! An alarm went off, and the machine started spitting out tickets. The alarm wouldn't go off so I had to get an employee. The machine ran out of tickets, so the guy had to go get a roll of tickets to put into the machine.

Me and Ron stood there waiting for him. The alarm just went off non stop until the guy came back, reloaded the machine, and Ron got all his tickets. I thought it was pretty cool he beat the game.

Dogs are pretty cool

Me and Onyx, Tom's all black pitbull, would always go to Penny Pack park. We would play in the shallow waters. I would bring my radio and everything. One time I brought the ipod. I let it play randomly. I didn't fast forward any of the songs. We walked deeper and deeper into the woods. I had one of the leashes that could extend out real far. The dog was sniffing the ground as he walked around. He turned left off the trail onto a smaller trail. We went through some trees. When we got to the other side, there was this enchanting beach.

There was a black snake sitting on top of this colossal tree branch sticking out of the water. The snake was pretty fat! My dad warned me about the snakes. There was a branch that came out of the ground and curved back into the ground. It was like a little bench. The trees leaves draped over the beach. I don't think the trees were weeping willows. It was just the way they grew into the ground. If you looked to the left the water was running over rocks and it was sunny. If you looked to the right the water was dark, still, and it was shady. I sat down on the tree branch bench. The exact moment my butt touched the branch the song "Whirlwind through Cities by Afura" came on. I felt really weird because the timing was quite unusual. When Tom and me were listening to this song in the car, he turned to me and said, "it's you." When we finally left the secluded beach, song 54 came on the ipod. It was Sade (By your side).

Work history

Volvo (2007)

I was a receptionist at Volvo in Langhorne. There was a guy named Brian. It was his birthday so I faxed the radio station we had playing in the showcase room. In the fax I explained that it was Brian's birthday. The radio station actually said something about his birthday. I wasn't there but Brian told me it played on the radio. Someone at another job used to always email her favorite radio station. So she was the one who gave me the idea. Like I said before you can learn anywhere you go.

Dominos Pizza

I found Tuesday Morning by driving around delivering pizzas for Dominos. I ended up working at Tuesday Morning for two years. That is a long time for me. My friend Peggy delivered pizzas and made out pretty good. She gave me the idea. This place just opened up so it was pretty slow because people still needed to find out about it. People told me to be careful because some pizza deliverers get robbed.

Bensalem Country Club (2000-2001)
This was a catering job. We did baby showers, weddings, all kinds of parties.

Tuesday Morning (2007-2009)

In college my email or my instant messenger name was Purplestar399. My friends at college would laugh at me because of it. When I worked at Tuesday Morning, something told me to look for a purple star. I would look at all the stuff we had and I seen a soccer ball. It had a big purple star on it. I turned the box it was in and seen the price. It was 3.99. I thought that was kind of weird. What was strange was the message in the middle of the purple star. It said, "It's a thin girl." What the heck is that supposed to mean!

I liked the music they played there. I don't know what they play in the store now.

All the women who checked out had their nails done. Every single woman.

I remember this one lady who checked out. She asked me, "What field are you in?" I said, "What do you mean?" She said, "You look like you are in the arts." I walked her to the door. I said, "I am in left field. I am way out there." She walked out the door. My boss looked at me and we shared a smile.

You can find the weirdest stuff there. There was a Barbie doll. I don't know if it was a Barbie doll. It was a doll of the same height and build. The theme of the doll was "Birds." The doll had lots of black birds on her. If you never heard of the movie "Birds" you will not get this. It also had a doormat that said, "Yo!"

Robin Hood

Sundays are Crazy there! They are some tough waitresses, cooks, dishwashers, and hosts! When I worked at Robin Hood, I worked at Tuesday Morning too. They were in the same mall strip. The waitress's (Robin Hood) birthday was March 1st. My boss's (Tuesday Morning) daughter's birthday was March 3rd. Theresa was the waitress's name. She was crazy. Crazy in a good way. She was hilarious. Stephanie was my boss at Tuesday Morning. She was real cool. Real cool. Stephanie's daughter Mariah was a great artist. The first time I seen her work was this time I was in Stephanie's office. When Stephanie showed me Mariah's work, I got Goosebumps on my arms. It was really good.

Home Depot (2005)

A guy called the store and asked for me. He wanted to take me out. I had a boyfriend at the time. I remember having a conversation with my co-worker there. I told him I have a degree in Computer Engineering. He was telling me he had a really good job before he came to Home Depot. He said that he doesn't make a lot of money at Home Depot. He said, "I don't go home with headaches when my shift is over." Behind him were the cash registers. Cash registers 5 and 4 were behind him. Only their lights were on.

Escort

I had to buy heels so I got heels from Joyce Leslie. These heels killed my feet. My feet were aching with pain. I had to call the client to confirm the appointment. The driver would always yell at me because he said I sounded like a drill sergeant. We would spend a lot of time sitting in the car and waiting for calls. When I decided to do it, it was real slow. I tried to keep it a secret but I bought dresses with the money I made. The dresses were a little too sexy. I stopped doing it because I really liked Richard and I didn't want to give him a disease. Me and Richard weren't boyfriend and girlfriend at the time. We were just messing around. I did it for 2 weeks. My first week, I sat in the car and learned how to book calls. I didn't do any calls the first week.

The one girl told me that there was a serial killer in New York who targeted prostitutes. One girl's client locked her in a room and wouldn't let her out. I don't know who was involved but I do know they tried to negotiate with the client for a while.

Dream

In this dream, I am in an evil place. It doesn't look creepy or anything but I knew it was an evil place. There are people around but I know better to approach them because everyone is evil as well. It was the kind of dream I was aware I was dreaming so I tried to wake myself up because I wanted to get out of this scary place. As hard as I tried to wake myself up, I couldn't. After awhile, I had a memory. I do not remember what the memory was but I do know it had to do with love. Once I had that memory and felt love because of it, I woke right up.

Once upon a time

I danced on Easter in a club called fluid. The song I danced to was called Sixth Sense. The music got so loud. I blacked out. There was only two people on the dance floor including me. I probably looked like an idiot, but I do remember one thing that caught my attention. <u>I froze.</u> I was behind the other girl. My legs were positioned like I was about to fight (a lunge). My torso was about 45 degrees to the floor. My arms reached out to her with my fingers spread apart. I didn't move. I stayed there. She eventually turned around to look at me. It's like a chain reaction. As soon as she turned to look at me, I started to dance again. I think Common is the artist of that song.

Selah

Ghost Stories

My mother saw a nun standing next to her bedroom door when she was a little girl.

My mother was in the upstairs bathroom in my grandmother's house. She heard someone run up the stairs and knock on the door three times. She was in the middle of curling her hair. She said, "Hold on." She thought it was my brother Luke. She opened the door. No one was there. She was scared and went downstairs and sat in the living room. When Luke came home she asked him if he stopped home earlier that day. He said that he never came home that day.

I would like to dedicate this book to
Rusha Reid

In the whole world,
There is only one of you . . .

My mom bought me a knick knack when I was little. It
had this message on it. ☺

Today is:

"One doesn't discover new lands without consenting to lose sight of the shore for a very long time."

-Andre Gide-